Lois E. Mikkelson

Library of Congress Catalog Card Number: 65-11582

Printed in the United States of America

2 3 4 5

LET'S FIND OUT ABOUT

ABRAHAM LINCOLN

by

MARTHA AND CHARLES SHAPP

pictures by James Caraway

FRANKLIN WATTS, INC.

575 Lexington Avenue, New York 22

Abraham Lincoln was one of the greatest
  presidents the United States ever had and one
  of the greatest men that ever lived.
He will always be remembered as the man who
  freed four million people from slavery.

Abraham Lincoln was born in Kentucky on
    February 12, 1809.
Like many other pioneer families of that time,
    the Lincolns lived in a log cabin.

When Abe was a little boy, the Lincolns moved
to Indiana.
To get to their new home, Mr. and Mrs.
Lincoln, Abe, and his sister, Sarah, traveled
miles and miles through thick forest.
And deep in the woods Mr. Lincoln built a
cabin for his family.

Abe was then only seven years old, but he was
tall and strong enough to use an ax.
Abe helped his father cut down the trees and
clear the land.

When Abe was nine years old, his mother died.
Abe and his sister were very sad children.
Sarah had to keep house for her father and
brother.

A year later, Mr. Lincoln married a widow with
   three children.
Abe's stepmother was a very kind woman.
She loved all five children.
The Lincolns were a happy family.

Abe had very little chance to go to school.

Schools in that part of the country were few and far between.

When Abe was eleven, a school was built near his home.

His stepmother thought education was important and Abe started school.

But he couldn't go very often.

He was needed at home to help with the work on the farm.

Altogether he had less than a year of school.

He learned to read and write and do a little arithmetic.

His love of reading started then and continued all through his life.

Abe was liked by everybody.
He was a good storyteller.
The boys and men in the neighborhood loved
   to listen to Abe's stories and jokes.

Abe grew very, very tall and thin, but he was
very strong.

He was always growing too big for his clothes.

Once, a big, heavy bully thought that he could
beat tall, thin Abe.

But Abe won the fight.

When the fight was over, the two men shook
hands and became friends.

Young Abe Lincoln had to work to help his
parents.

Sometimes, he worked for twenty-five cents a
day.

At night he read and practiced writing and
arithmetic.

He didn't always have pencil and paper.

Sometimes he had to write with charcoal on a
shovel.

Abe read every book he could get.
One day he borrowed a book from a neighbor.
Before he went to bed, he put the book away
between two logs in the wall.

It rained that night.

The book was badly damaged.

Abe asked the man what he could do to pay
for the damage.

The man said that Abe would have to work for
three days.

After Abe had done the work, the man gave
the book to Abe to keep.

Once Abe took a job on a flatboat that went all
   the way down the Mississippi River.
There, in the South, he saw slaves forced to
   work for their masters.
Lincoln was shocked.

For a time, Abe worked in a store.

When there were no customers, he stretched out on the counter and read.

One day, by mistake, Abe gave a customer less tea than she had paid for.

That night Abe walked many miles to bring the rest of the tea to the customer.

Perhaps his nickname "Honest Abe" started at that time.

Abraham Lincoln made friends wherever he
   went.
He was gentle and kind to everybody.
Abe often read the newspapers to people who
   could not read.

Lincoln decided to study law.

He borrowed law books and studied hard.

In 1836 he became a lawyer.

In those days, lawyers traveled from town to
town to try their cases.

Lincoln became known to many people.

When he ran for Congress, the people elected
him.

Lincoln was a fine speaker.

He began to speak out against the spread of
slavery in the United States.

People all over the country heard about
Abraham Lincoln and his speeches.

In 1860 the people who were against slavery
chose Abraham Lincoln to run for president
of the United States.

The people in the southern states where slaves
   were kept did not want Lincoln for president.
They said that if Lincoln were elected, they
   would no longer consider themselves part of
   the United States.
Lincoln was elected and eleven southern states
   did try to leave the Union.
These states formed a new country called the
   Confederate States of America.
Southern soldiers fired on a United States fort.
The Civil War had begun.

Battle after battle was fought.
Sometimes the North won, sometimes the South
   won.
But the war went on and on.

In 1864, Abraham Lincoln was reelected president.

Soon after, the North won and the war was over.

The war had done a great deal of damage to the country, especially to the South.

Lincoln wanted to do everything possible to help the country recover from the war.

Lois E. Mikkelson

But he didn't get the chance.
Five days after the war ended, Abraham
    Lincoln was shot and killed.

The people of America built a beautiful
Memorial in Washington, D.C., to honor
Abraham Lincoln.

Every day people from all over the world visit
the Lincoln Memorial to honor the man who
lived and died for the freedom of all people.

VOCABULARY

a
Abe ('s)
about
Abraham
after
against
all
altogether
always
America
an
and
announcement
arithmetic
as
asked
at
away
ax

badly
battle
be
beat
beautiful
became
bed
before
began
begun
between
big
book (s)
born
borrowed
boy (s)
bring
brother
built
bully
but

by

cabin
called
cases
cents
chance
charcoal
children
chose
Civil War
clear
clothes
Confederate
Congress
consider
continued
could (n't)
counter
country
customer (s)
cut

damage (d)
day (s)
deal
decided
deep
did (n't)
died
do
done
down

education
elected
eleven
Emancipation
    Proclamation
ended
enough

especially
ever
every
everybody
everything

families
family
far
farm
father
February
few
fight
fine
fired
five
flatboat
for
forced
forest
formed
fort
fought
four
free (d)
freedom
friends
from

gave
gentle
get
go (ing)
good
great (est)
grew
growing

had
hands
happy

hard
have
he
heard
heavy
help (ed)
her
him
his
home
honest
honor
house

if
important
in
Indiana
it

January
job
jokes

keep
Kentucky
kept
killed
kind
known

land
later
law
lawyer (s)
learned
leave
less
life
like (d)
Lincoln (s)

44

listen
little
lived
log (s)
longer
love (d)

made
man
many
married
masters
memorial
men
miles
million
Mississippi
mistake
mother
moved
Mr.
Mrs.

near
needed
neighbor (hood)
new
newspapers
nickname
night
nine
no
North
not

of
often
old
on
once
one
only

other
out
over

paid
paper
parents
part
pay
pencil
people
perhaps
pioneer
possible
practiced
president (s)
put

rained
ran
read (ing)
recover
reelected
remembered
rest
river
run

sad
said
Sarah
saw
school (s)
seven
she
shocked
shook
shot
shovel
sister
slavery
slaves

soldiers
sometimes
soon
south (ern)
speak (er)
speeches
spread
started
states
stepmother
still
store
stories
storyteller
stretched
strong
studied
study

tall
tea
than
that
the
their
themselves
then
there
these
they
thick
thin
those
thought
three
through
time
to
too
took
town
traveled

trees
try
twenty-five
two

Union
United States
use

very
visit

walked
wall
want (ed)
war
was
Washington
way
went
were
what
when
where
wherever
while
who
widow
will
win
with
woman
won
woods
work (ed)
world
would
write
writing

year (s)
young

Lois E. Mikkelson